THOMAS CORY MYERS

a beautiful place…

When I found you, I found a way to a beautiful place…

-You-

Can you drive through the city? Can you catch a falling star? Can you paint the words to describe who you are? To a river and a rainbow. On the mountain, through a meadow. I close my eyes to see through clouds into the sky.

-Spirits-

We are the spirits of man-kind. Whatever we do, we leave behind and other people see it too. That is why it is good to do something true; to show that we believe in you. Always seek to find the truth. Remember good times of your youth. Did you behave when you went to school? Learn a trade or two.

-Special-

It's good to carry your charms with you. Everywhere you go the special things around you are part of you, you know, and gifts from family or from friends are especially priceless. The love that gives never ends. Do unto others as you would have them do unto you. Give them something as individual as you.

-Four-

Old and rightfully new. Earth laid garments. The sky returns to blue from blackness seeking light. Creation. Out of sight. Far away. Looking at myself as I'm writing and comparing two and two.

-Survive-

Life is one chance to stay alive and beat the rest. Survival of the fittest and the test of time. Survival of your mind. If you talk too much you take away. If you don't talk at all you're no fun anyway. Keep it simple what you have to say. Be important. Don't stand in the way.

-Here's the Lighter, Fire Fighter-

Do not be the fool, for one wrong move might throw you for a loop. Watch and listen and see where you place your foot upon each step. To hurry is not the right way, unless you really need to get away. To start off, you have to take it slow. Later on, you can run.

-Create-

Don't say a word. Save it 'til the time is there. You will know. Relax and stare. Things will come to you, in time, to tell you what you need to do. It's what and all that is inside of all of you.

-Bridge-

Don't burn all your bridges or you won't be able to mend it. To see your friends and family is one of the greatest things to be. If you are being followed or something wants to bring you pain, burn that bridge, never to return again. Climbing up the ladder, it really doesn't matter where you are. Keep a look upon a star, a boiling sun or one so far. Try to find out which star you are. Believe in yourself, then what you can do and see how far that will take you.

-Labels-

When you carve your name into a tree, you label that tree of what *you* could be. Now who will come and label me? Just accept who you are and know that labels don't mean a thing. We just keep on growing. We all want to be free.

-Practice-

Practice makes perfect. Know what you want to do, but always remember to do what you need to. You have to or you will be fed to; weak and weary to see through.

-Rest-

A true believer in yourself is to become what you think is best for you and no-one else, but always remember a time of rest. Sleep. Breathe in. Take a deep breath. Now relax and calm yourself. Peace at last. To be in silence; to be at ease, as softly as a gentle breeze.

-Build-

Breathing, breathing. Slip back again, as easily as I did begin. As many sounds that are from within and all around, to be content. Where are you? Surrounded? Find a place to live in that you will love and always give. That begins a home. To will what you say, not say what you will. If you are going to build, then build and then at last when the work is done, turn around and live and love. For your hard work will pay off, but you've got to do it right. If it gets tough then continue to fight. For labor builds yourself and mind. To make you feel strong and learn your way of doing things. To take and use for everyday and teach someone in some strange way.

-Gifts-

If you give it away, then it's gone. So know what you show and who will cherish what you let go the most.

-The City-

Plain of the wind, blowing through the grain and a man walking amongst the rain, that sinks into his shirt and the city scrambling, rambling changes in every direction. A new retrospective and noises and sounds and insects and ravens and stocks and rounds and pillow fights and clowns. Neatly etched, for one bright speck, upon this space that spins and slips into a race of rats nestled in a maze.

-Experience-

Why do you sit in your cupboards? Why not try and discover new things? Instead of relying on man-made things that surely collapse. So easily, I laugh. Don't you know who is made of stone and who will make a clone and then which man has one who's alive yet and who's been born yet? Get with the times, man. I'm so bored! So stop your yelling. Don't ignore what you're spelling. Find something that you think is bad and destroy it without getting it mad. Love your neighbor as thyself. Keep thy seal upon thy chest. Guard your life and what you have left. For the children, they are born. Hear them cry. That child is about to begin a whole new experience.

-Home Sweet Home-

I will ride through the range, through the wild and the strange. I will hold to the dream that I know. I will walk each day though I'll never be the same. I must go on until I make it back home. As I cross over the plain, through the wind and the rain, my dreams tell me where I need to go and the strings that I play, I can almost hear them say, "Lead me to my home sweet home."

-How it's Been-

Mama, let me tell ya how it's been. Many roads I've traveled over again. I'm here on the mountain and I'm doing fine and I love you as the sun loves the sky. The birds keep singing a sweet lullaby as I lay here dreaming on the hillside. I love you and I'm gonna try to be a good boy 'til the day that I die. Nothing will ever keep us apart. Our love keeps on growing how near or far. I love you, that's for sure. I'll love you, forevermore.

-Down on the Farm-

And the world lets you go on and after the song is sung we'll go riding…into the sun and find a home right here in our hearts and write a song down on the farm. And the world helps you to go on and after the song is sung we'll go riding…into the sun.

-Mountain Home Place-

This mountain is my home place, a shelter from the storm. This mountain is my childhood, from the time that I was born. This mountain is my teacher, who helps me as a friend. This mountain is my freedom that never has an end. This mountain is my wonder, in the twinkling of an eye. This mountain will be my tombstone on the day that I will die. This mountain is my message, my words, and my songs. This mountain is my family. This mountain is my home. Oh, make me a home on a mountain of stone, deep in the rolling hills, by the waterfall. As I sit upon this Stone Mountain face, I think about my own, mountain home place.*

*CO-WRITTEN BY: DANNY ROYALL

10

-Darn-

It's not too late to mend the things you break. It's not too late to change the path you take. Just, hold on to what you know is true and find the one to give your lovin to.

-Little Log Cabin-

In a little log cabin, in the woods on a mountain. By a crooked little stream, where you let yourself dream. Let your thoughts drift away on a bright sunny day. You could lose your mind when you're in the moonshine. Well, the chickens need a feedin and the fields need a plowin. The cows need a milkin and the dogs are a howlin. Choppin wood all day, 'cause winter's on the way. With a woman like mine, I'm a doing just fine.

-True-

Well, times can be hard. You've got to be smart and listen to your heart. If you don't try to understand, you never will. I know how you feel. Find love and you will find a true friend. I will help you if I can. Well, times can be rough. You've got to be tough and give enough. Do you believe me when I say, I want to love you every day and always be true for you? I want to love you right. I want to hold you every-night and I want to say, I want to love you every-day and always be true for you.

-Reflect-

I could live in this moment forever, but returning is how I feel alive. You know how we love this sunny weather and when the cold winds blow you must survive. Struggling to reach the destination. Trying not to waste any more time. In the sun you can see your reflection. How many hills have you climbed?

-A Voice-

When I sat and thought quietly still, I sensed the sound of silence. When there was a spot for filling, I listened for their answers. They, puzzled, looked for me to fill this meaning and when I returned and started to speak, I found it hard to talk. To capture what you're really feeling. To get in all your thoughts. Every insight to every question was the thought of all discussion. As though you could answer anything and anything was your final answer. To ever speak. To say a word into the sound that is the world and then you found that when a voice is louder than its words, then it cannot be heard.

-Old Time Station-

Sittin down here at the Old Time Station. Tryin to catch a ride. Don't know the destination. Just a waitin to get on down the tracks. Lord knows, I ain't ever comin back. Well, I'm long gone. Going to meet my maker. Gonna make this trip my own. No mistakin, I'm gone. Just a movin on right along. See ya later, gotta go, so long. Well, I'm a hollerin and a dancin and a shakin and a screamin and groovin and a singin a song. Sayin, today is the day, oh lordy, I'm gonna fly away. I ain't got no money, honey. Don't need it anyway. No way. Gonna ride this train. Gonna ride it away. Until I get to that place where I can stay.

-One Family-

We'll always be together. We're all one family. Let's love each other in sweet harmony and share all our dreams, that we bear of our names and tell our childhood legends. Sitting by the fireside, playing our music. We dance and sing. We'll always be together. We're all one family. Let's love each other. Let yourselves be free. Laying in the moonlight, watching the fire die. We share our dreams. We'll always be together.*

*CO-WRITTEN BY: SHAWN ROSE

-Time and Ease-

Love is all you really need and faith in the Lord above. Share and believe, all you really need is love. Life is a blessing. Never knowing how you'll find things. To help you realize what it's all for. Time and ease, help you open up the door. All you see will never be as before.

-Relation Ships-

I've been back to the outer regions. The place where it's hard to look back and I willingly led myself this way to find true meaning. Time plays the important part in this, yet every moment is changing with new meaning. The truth is plain to see. The future is never knowing. Hope in all things and strength in your self-will can help you. Guidance through specific meaning that can finally be understood. One step ahead, the only obtainable answer. With every step and decision, you make your idea what it is. Your success is controlling yourself mainly and, as well, the situation itself. You make it through by allowance and proof of character, which is just being yourself and your word aloud, held up to your accounted action. Correctly show the world yourself and your place, wherever it should be. By the only way, go out and do something that is entirely you, knowing full well that you can…if you try. Our relationships should not be based on the troubles around us. It should be based on why we are together in the first place.

-Roll Away-

I seem so lost, yet so long ago I pictured this. You see, all you got is one thing and the future is another. Who knows either way many things could decide. All we really did was take a ride, you know, on the open road. I really love the way we roll. Well, just keep on rolling that's one thing. All you got, so just roll. So many paths and so many things. Find the right way; *your* way and see where it takes you. What you'll find is what you really need and goodbye ain't so easy. Just roll away.

-A Part-

You might as well just say goodbye. At least that would be a reason why. You'd have to leave and follow the tide and who knows where the sea will ride. The only hope that I might see, would be to see your ship sail next to me, again. Because even though the sea is wide and the road is long, you could be right by my side and this world could be quite small. Once you have seen, you can never part. Once in a dream or maybe in your heart. In this sea we are all together. For now we are just apart.

-The Saint Marie-

The ship is sailing down the stairs. The waning moon left dust in the trail and all you could hear was the song of the whale. Wind and storms and wrath of sea, could not destroy the Saint Marie. The crew and mast both equal in strength. The Saint Marie would never sink. Many would say or hear the tale, that the Saint Marie was setting sail and all you could hear was the song of the whale. A ship to fight the wars of sea. Long live the queen, Her Majesty. When waves get rough as they can be, there would be the Saint Marie.

Steady the wheel and raise the sail and all you could hear was the song of the whale.

-Spell Bound-

Unearthed monuments of eternity. Guardian of the ages. With a watchful eye. Soul of the material world. Spell bound. Creating in design. Between two mountains. The morning construction of the sunrise. From beyond symbolic. Somewhere deep in the valley. New kingdom. New life. The sun and the rain. A meeting in the ancient realm. Silent. To come and go. Devoted. A gate to the other world.

-Your Place in Time-

You will find your place in time. I follow you, your sun does shine. Save yourself, then save your mind. Leave the rest, leave it all behind. Take your time. Take it easy. Watch the day go flying by. It's alright. It ain't easy. You don't know what you'll find. Everything was just fine, until the rain fell from the sky and now I often wonder why. Get up. Get on. Get out the door. Get on your way.

-A Sparkling Glimmer-

As you sit all alone, in the woods by a river, on a log. Looking at a sparkling glimmer. A glimpse of it all. Here in the forest of nature, our dreams are real. Free to escape in wondering. A long endless night. Dance with me sweet angel, angel of light. Look at the creatures upon the floor, gathering to be once more. All together, in a dream. All together, you and me. Love her until your dying day. All together, you will stay. Love her, she will bring you luck. Love is the key which opens the lock. Look her in the eye. Tell her that you want to fly away to a fairytale dream, confusing as it may be. All is safe if you're with me, look around and see.

-Seasonal Waves-

Half by chance and half by reason. Shifting to another season. The world that gives, will take away. Changing, amazing. Only by chance could there be such a fate. A constant slip that is never the same. In and out of space. Listening to the change. Watching the waves constantly repeating the same old thing in many different ways.

-Sometimes-

Sometimes, it's hard to see. Sometimes, it's hard to believe. Sometimes, we all have a need. Sometimes, we fight to be free. Sometimes, there are no words. Sometimes, we follow the herd. Sometimes, we just don't care. Sometimes, it's just not fair. Sometimes, we cannot speak. Sometimes, we prey on the weak. Sometimes, we hold you high. Sometimes, we spread our wings and say goodbye. Sometimes, you see it coming. Sometimes, it just slips away. Some ways, there are warnings. Some days, it just might rain. There is no way of knowing. So think it through the change. Sometimes, you make it right and tomorrow might be the day and I might forget what I was going to say…

-A Learning Process-

It's always a learning process. A speck of dust on the wall. An answering machine at a birthday party. Ride into the future of multi-perception. Climb a dark mountain to be the first to see the sunrise. Futuristic fantasy. The ultimate guide to your own interpretation. Be yourself, I guess. Whatever that means.

-A Maze-

It amazes you and you don't know what to say or do. When it's done then you're through to something else that amazes you. What do I have to do? I have to keep amazing you? It amazes you to see something new. Give me a moment and I'll see what I can do. I just want you to see me through. I have to keep amazing you.

-Mountainside-

Love is so strange. When you know that every-day is going to change. On a mountainside, I will call your name. How did things end up this way? I will try to reach you, through the clouds and the rain. But, I know that it's so hard when you're so far away. Oh, I know that it's alright for me to feel this way. I know that the sun will shine each day and I know that I'll find a way through to you.

-Sun through the Rain-

Sun through the rain. A diamond in the mist. Light from a thousand rainbows, you just can't miss. Well, I've seen the mountainside and I've climbed the hill. I've looked for the other side, but it seems so far from here. Now, you remind me that the sun shines every day. The light that hides behind a cloud will shine through the rain. Sun through the rain. Wash away my pain. What else can I say? If there's a will then there's a way to find the sun through the rain.

-Freedom Rings-

The house built with sin will hold up long, but shall crumble at the feet of denial. And existence is explained as a fairytale. When lies and hate build a community, the sanction is broken and in it forms the birth of society. Breeding the strong. Beseeching the unholy. A formidable arrangement of colors and lines. Freedom rings, but freedom is a license for chaos.

-The Voyage-

Signs, posted on the wall. The words dance out at you, as you expect to see through the wall. Do you wish you had the upper hand? Look around. Be quick if you can and always remember to help the other man. Listen. Listen to him. It hurts me too, you know, thinking about good old times, when life turns around and hands you lies. We are all born alive, into a world with one great sky. We're all afloat on one grand sea. The boat will rock, but don't let it sink. Do you know where you need to go? Plan the voyage. Prepare for the unknown and who knows, maybe one day…land ho!

-Stock-

Buy it low and sell it high. Pick a flower, and then watch it die. The key to anyone's recipe is to plant, then wait and see. I take what I know and remember to sow the best looking seed. To keep on growing and watch out for the weeds. Snow, sun, rain or hail. I don't know, I just can't tell.

-Out of Sight-

Listen to the spirits, they will guide you, but only you will know what is right for you. Respect your elders, past and present. Ask for guidance and you just might get it. Don't sweat it. Just try and forget it. Think aloud, but don't disrespect it. Look again. Step within. Remember where to begin and end. If that's not right, jump, flash, gone. Then, out of mind is out of sight.

-Where Two Waters Meet-

Sitting where two waters meet, a man is fishing. In the air a bird is flying, thinking of a clear blue sky. They look at each other and know they are brothers. Fishing or flying home, and they kindly say goodbye.

-Ghost of Man-

Do you see an Indian or a ghost on the roof or a man who is walking too close to you telling you what you already knew? You are here in my perception and guide me in my general direction. To look at my past, I keep leaving behind and following truth, to see what I'll find. I am here now and so are you. I will lead or follow you through. I am free to conclude. We walk the strait and narrow, towards the sun and moon. A clashing silence brought us to anew. What we can do is misunderstood by many, but few are aware and may even try to scare a new face onto you. Stay in your place you lowly disgrace. Your masters are too aware of you. Trapped in a basement that is all your own. You want to know. You know I can't tell you. You don't believe me? Can't you see what's happening to you? Watch the world that is around you. Look what we can do together. Save the world and this awful weather. Let's see spring and leaves of green. The sun is shining bright, brighter than you could ever believe. We stick together in clubs or clans. In garbage cans if we have to. Relish the sun. It's such a delight to be in this spring that we're not used to. The future of a sky so blue. I love it. Don't you? I'm not who you think I am. We are together forever.

-Rollin-

Rollin...rollin along. Movin your feet to the sound of the song. Got to keep rollin on. You gotta find...a reason to live. I said, you've gotta find...a reason to live. Give it all, as much as you know. By the looks of it, well, it's time to roll. There's one more thing I think you should know. I say, your life, babe, ain't just for show. You got to find...a reason to live. Give it all, as much as you know. By the looks of it, well, it's time to roll. Roll, baby, roll. Ride along...ride along.

-It Goes to Show-

You know, it goes to show how much faith we have in each other, for another besides our own.

If you see him all alone, who will cast the first stone at your brother or someone that you might have known? Oh why, oh why, do we waste our time diggin on someone else's hole? Well, it's safe to say, that I'll be o.k. all on my own. And it always seems that no-one understands a thing. We just go on and think about what we might have done. Well, you used to assume that you knew what to do from your first step, until your last and from then on.

-Tomorrow-

Tomorrow we shall go to a land that we don't know and everyone will dance and sing, I don't know what tomorrow brings…

-Lullaby-

The rains came and the mornings flew by. Still I wait to see the day, the look within your eye. And when that day came, the sun was in the sky. Everyone that I could see was part of me, somewhere deep inside. A bird came, to sing a lullaby and tell me that I'm free to be, free to leave, or free to fly.

-Oh, Well-

Step into a cloud. Racing to the rainbow. Got to get out of here. Where do you go? Well, do you know when it's the right time of year? Slipping through the sunlight. Gathering all the rain. Tell me what I might hear. You know, it might be hell in the bottom of a well, but at least I have you near.

-The Castle will Fall-

Is there more of that, to this? You know, it's something that you just can't miss. Well, you came upon a castle and ran into a hassle and got into some trouble again. The party seemed to breakdown, the walls began to shakedown and the world began to crawl to a halt. On the dawning of a new day, you try to make your get-away, but you always seem to get caught. Time to get on. Of many things you have no need.

-A Chance-

Life is grand. Life is what you make it. Can you understand what to give or when to take it? Life is a chance to learn from your mistakes. Will you

see the day when there is no more to make? Know we got to slow down. Got to get my feet back on the ground. Don't tell me where you're going. Don't tell me where you've been. The only thing that matters now is what you're standing in. Say, you had a friend. He would not understand. He turned around and turned you out and said you don't fit in. But, who was there to lend a helping hand? Did you give him the slightest chance?*

*CO-WRITTEN BY: DONESE STULTZ

-Blend-

On the other side, see your friends go rolling by. You know, I had a real great time. I think we'll meet again, alright. In my mind are memories so often kind, but a loss came from deep inside. To lose a friend, to leave behind. Not yet, do I regret a single thing. To me this means everything. What you feel is what you say. Everyone should feel this way. To blend a home, a family name. If we go or if we stay, we're all together anyway.

-For All to See-

Finally, it's what I needed. A chance to slip away to another day. Back again, that good old feeling. One that I have grown to love. It's one you'll find in the most unlikely places. You wake from your thoughts as you pass through this dream, for all to see.

-Fire-

A tremble. A force. A fire. All at once surging through you. Awakened in plain view. You remember now. But, what exactly was it? Some dream of a childhood memory you hold forever or a sudden yearning of what you will always want to hold? You must reach for something and release it all. For one will always remember and understand true feelings and love is a good word not to use lightly. Love makes one. Love takes two. What is life without it? Alone. Out.

-Unwind-

The sun is rising over the sea. To me, you are the reason the sun keeps shining. And there you are, you hold the keys to my heart and the world keeps unwinding. No, we don't know how long we can go on. The only way that we get by, is the love that we hold inside and you give it all away. It's in all the words that you feel that you've got to say. It's what we try so hard to find and try even harder when we say goodbye. But I know, lord I know, one thing will remain. And that is love, sweet love, love will never change and you give it all away.

-Balance-

Living to know what you see. Here we are passing time away. From ancient times until now we see the same change. New winds and winding passages. Over hills and under old mountains. Red berries in spring. A slight "hello" of the dew in the morning. An old branch hangs over the creek and stretches to the other side. Running across, arms wide. Gliding, amidst tests of inner peace. A release of your mind. Of everything…and that's when you'll know.

-Rio Grande-

Going to the country, by the Rio Grande. Everybody's coming along. I don't know how far

'til we get there.   If we even get there at all.
Dance all night in the cool moonlight.   Every-
body's singing a song.   Way out in the woods and
watching the stars.   Somebody said, it wouldn't be
too hard to pack up your things and get into the
car and let's drive to the country, by the Rio
Grande.   Everybody's singing along.   I don't know
how far 'til we get there.   If we even get there at
all.

-I Don't Know Anything-

Live endless words of wisdom.   Send every
thought to the world.   You will find out an inkling
of what you're really here for and what you're
supposed to be.   There is no sense to be had.   You
make it up as you go along, even a pre-paved
instance.   Every bit of life is completely what you
make it.   Though often hard, changing, relentless
growth so uncontrolled by your mind and yet it is
seemingly a miracle of harmony and you attribute
to it.   So you seldom stay in one place for too
long.   You get through to these moments of
peace.   A world of complete wonder that can be
ground.   Taking these moments to write them
down.   Anything *is*, but a great feeling *is* more apt
to be drawn.   What do you want to know?   That's
a good question because you may never find it.
Surrender to reality only to defy it around every

turn. Restlessness. Harmony is when you don't think or even know anything at all.

-Wind-

I stood in a field where I let myself go and listen for the wind to blow. Smokey hills. On a mountain. Our time. I see you are just as the wind and its breezes. Oh, so many replacements and cries of pages unturned, untold. Ripples of time unfold. A bird on a mountain. Your wings spread wide, you turn and you fly away. Over the land and over the sea. In a field, over-watching everything. By and by. Just as the wind and its breezes.

-Butterfly-

Sitting on a bridge with my feet in the water. Looking around, I see a beautiful sky and a butterfly lands gracefully on a flower beside me. Drifting into my thoughts of another day. My love will be here soon, on this warm afternoon, to sit with me for another day. Such a wonderful feeling, filled with so much meaning. I've waited my whole life to be here with you, for another day.

-Blue Stars-

Blue stars. Birds flying. One day, a memory of all things. A message in a stranger's warm-full touch. Wandering, drifting, and growing on the Earth. Carried away into the skies and mountain streams. The old times and laughter that brings flight in the evening, throughout the morning. In the words of a glimpse or waiting to say goodbye. Stop and look at each other. Take me there, passing places once remembered. Time awareness. Strength and silence. Tightening the harness. Hills, valleys, plains, paths, direction. Resting a bit. Smiles and a certain song we all know. Leaving late. Running behind the dark clouds. Chasing the light of moon-lit passages.

-Gypsy Girl-

Gypsy girl, in your world. Through your eyes, a star white pearl. With her head held so high, a tree grows to meet the sky and flowers reach for your hand. In your ship, you sail through this fairytale, in a world of many lands. The words came to you in your dreams. Everything that you see is surrounded by what you cannot seem to see, until you get there, to that somewhere…

-Nature Boy-

There is a boy who lives in the woods, wandering through the trees. By a stream, in a daydream. By the waterfall, listening to mother nature call, with words, throughout the breeze. Taking his time. Flowing with ease. He'll play a tune for you and he'll play one for me. And he sings all day long. Listen to the words in his song, of the forest of many trees.

-One by One-

I love you, but in a sad song way. Remember the moments. Remember the day. One by one, they fade away. In my heart I feel the same, but everywhere there is change. Lord only knows who is to blame. No paths or patterns. Just separate ways. I guess it had to be that way. Seasons change from light to grey. A bird, a star, a dream, like water through a stream, will finally meet the sea. So vast and distant indefinitely, but often times not what it seems.

-Remember This-

A gallant ship raising and waiting for tide. So they went walking. So quickly was I to stutter for the sake of all that's to be. Unknown and but a question of our own true destiny. Drifting, float away. Inside you hide at the brink of day. Suddenly, a shadows name. Something we missed along the way. Remembering that, it's not so far or maybe it is. Remember this.

-Long Bottom Blues-

A cozy autumn, down on Long Bottom. Carry me out to the sun, in the fields and spread me onto the hills, to wander around and over the sky and into the clouds. So I wander into you. There in the valley. So I dream the skies away and find the place to stay, as the seasons and the colors change. I wander without you, in silence. I listen to the wind. I stare into the sun. Speak of what you've seen. Tell me what you've learned.

-Unfold-

We look for beauty in our world. Through every movement and in every word. For when you find it and the secrets it holds, the colors begin swirling, as the flower unfolds. And when she speaks, will you hear what she'll say? As the world spins around for another day. High hopes and dreams. In the moment or even in a memory. What is hidden might be plain to see.

-Electric Sparks-

You are just electric sparks reaching for the arc across space. Make your own choices. Control your own life. Let your conscience be your guide. There is no limit within. On the bottom, top or middle, it really doesn't matter.

-Somewhere Shows-

At somewhere shows. In back rows and weathered stacks of blackened roads. In shells and homes, you know. Out there, beyond the air. Time and space. Anticipate. Flowered seeds of people's needs, on a world that spins around. In steps, through seasons. Beyond the reasons of threats or thoughts or dreams. A cast of beings. Delicate plates of serine. A green sea. To sleep there, together with her on a mountain. A rainbow shower and sunlight over seas and stones. Of many gardens grown.

-Clouds of Rain-

Have you seen the wondrous city that is growing towards the sky? To reach the sun they try. Wandering through the journey. Opening pathways. Carried along ways. Towards doorways. To the angel who sang to gather the clouds of rain. Watering the city, to wash the doubt away. Beautiful changing keys of melodies, throughout the breeze of uncertainties. The unknown force that sets the course. The many different sources that lead to the dreams in your head. To keep you moving ahead, though you are asleep in your bed.

-I Don't Mind-

I don't mind if I do. I don't mind if I don't. When I get through, I must go on. And no-body knew when it came to it all. But, you wrap your arms around me because I love you and that's plain to see. I'm going home, because that's the place to be. When I'm with you and you're here with me. But, it seems so hard to find the truth.

To know who we are. I don't mind, but I must go on.

-Responsibility-

Here we are to see the sacred universe. As all of everything moves by. Seen on walls, describing all of the thoughts of what we are. To be seen in the universe. Reaching forward. No periods of time, just moving, as though alive. A place of ours, our own, surrounded by all that's unknown. Contained in everything. All that is and is to be. A battle enforcing judgment, but essential in obtaining sight. Of all things obtained by sight, responsibility is most important.

-Empires-

Soft flicks of water predict rain. Drumming designs. Empires. In your hands, drawing dreams of shadows and stories told, tenderly. By the window, those chilling dark clouds keep moving close. From drizzle, to drops, to gust of rage and rain. Rumbling showers of thunder and power. Sliding to settle and then gone. Years ago, seems like yesterday. For kings and queens and mysterious beings. Shuffled and split and spent on the land. Slowly watching. Call across the road and lights in sight. Nothing. Looking.

-Mourning Dove-

My sweet love, it'll be alright. A mourning dove, soon to take her flight. All that surrounds her and all that's inside and steps that she will see, she will climb and soon soar to fly so high, around the moon and the setting sun sky. Above the ground, so lovely a sound as she comes gliding by. The winds carry her name over trees and rivers, to rolling waves of the sea. In a sunshine or standing there next to me.

-Last Funk-

All be those gathered together in one. Surrounded by the names of each conjoined. Every sound aloud. Every drop of rain. Every moment. Every time of place. Every pause…to see every sky, each as one. A moment in the ocean. So bright. The deeper we go within, the further we step outside. All be those together. Drifting away. Silent, no-one hears. Lost in the day. Seems like many years. Somewhere far away.

-Sequential Anguish-

Where are you? The other piece of myself? As I turn into a fading darkness, I climb upon the mountain, alone. Floating memories that construct the future. Changing and facing each moment. Staggering in the midst of the breeze. Growing towards a distant star. Rolling and moving, I wake from some magical dream, crying. I am searching for you always and everywhere I go you are not there. I feel desperation and resentment inside my mind. Into a sequential state of anguish, my sub-conscience screams for resolution. To the ends of the Earth, until nothing is left of myself except the essence of love, continuously flowing forever.

-Shadow-

Backwards glancing. Run around, swift and loud. Applause, broken off by the sound. Part of it all, centered along soft, offered sunlight. Sweet and laughing. Just sitting there, unaware, watching the breeze with a sense of ease. Lying in a field of flowers, counting clouds to relax. We stand up to fall down again. Into your hands, holding on forever. Look beneath; our shadows are one to be.

-Friend-

Washing away this poor discomfort. Weary, am I, in this cold weather. Waiting for the rain. A lonely tear springs forth, falling slowly to the floor. Inside, I lay still watching through my eyes. A friend comes walking to my side. "What is your fear?" he asks. I stumble and race through my mind to a picture unreal and thus far unseen. I don't know what it is that I fear. "Be calm," he says, "for I will always be here and love will save you from your fear. Open your heart and the rain will come to clean."

-The Little Flower-

Here we slow again. A center of a glimmer. Twisting into one. Turning of the soil. The seagull's wind, that turned and sent them into what wonder meant. Regaining speed again. Stepping back to see it. What the seed had brought them. A little flower, so strong and looking back to them. They smile and gather thoughts and talk and talk. Such a beautiful flower. He was on the right road indeed. And he loved the rain because it cleaned him and gave him nourishment. And he loved the sun because it showered him with more love than anything.

The flower just wanted to grow and grow to make the people even happier, but the flower was alone. Even though he had the sun, even though he had the rain, and even though he had the people he was still alone. He needed something else. So one magical day the people noticed the dismay and nurtured the flower night and day. He felt a little better and stood as tall as he could and then what do you know, here came the wind. It blew so gently and something came to him. He could sense a love. She was so close, but he could only feel her. Where could she be? The wind kept blowing harder than before and the man woke up and rushed to the door...

-News-

I don't need to know about it all the time. I'm always on my toes, never worried about my clothes. So you know it's time to go and get on with your lives. Don't listen to them tell you. Just listen to the news. Never let them fail you in knowing what to do. Keep playing your fiddle, in the light of the moon. A gentle floating spirit. A melody. A tune. So changing and then gone, but always soft to sooth. Here he comes again, to be my friend. We laugh, we smile and then we only grin and laugh out loud and spin into the wind.

-The Golden Book-

Looking at the golden book, the dust I scattered and then I shook and then it settled, as I lost one more petal. I gathered all my things together and left behind the rattled thistles. I'll see yaw later. I love you still, but you know we all have a place to fill. Inside your heart I know that we will never part. I'll be back one day, but the funny thing to say is, you'll find me.

-Waiting for the Show-

When the night seems so cold, you sit all alone, crying out to the Lord to help you go on. A war between two worlds. The battles carved in stone and an angel to guide us, to find another home. Castles in the mountains. Canyons filled with snow. The sorrow over-flowing, waiting for the show. A path with stars and many roads, leading up to another ending. The ones we think we know. Even though it's just beginning, spinning to and fro. Shadows calling out to you, to see within your soul.

-Fall into Winter-

Over the mountain, a million miles away. Slip into the shadows, until another day. The light from the cavern glows in the serpents eyes. The rain upon the rock. A spring that once was dry. The silence of the mist, following the stream. The forest is empty or so it may seem. The chill of the wind sets in for the night. The sky is on fire with brilliance and light. The snow is falling slowly. A secret from within. Fall into winter all over again.

-Patience-

Patience in yourself will always help you through. Wait and think before you do and try to know a little of what you're getting yourself into.

-Echo-

Fear is a word for un-wanting. Drink and be merry. The beat of your mind slips away into the night. I'm not leaving. Don't look behind. You echo your life's meaning.

-Dragonfly-

So, after the fighting and working is done. To sit and stare upon the sun, circling in motion. Always time to move along and weave yourselves through times to see. Maybe the answer is hanging from a tree. Pick the fruit and eat. From the best crop, find the best seed, to plant again in the time of your spring. Life and love in words of peace.

-One Pattern-

To the mountain across the sea. Through the clouds of mystery. Everywhere I go, I cast a shadow on the Earth. Since the time of my birth, life has put me to the test and you should expect no less. We choose each path we follow, on the straight and narrow, under the sun and moon. A shelter for the Earth. I see the angel's wings are raised to shine. As each moment passes by, the eagle flies by the sun. One pattern. We all choose the path we follow.

-High on the Hog-

High on the hog, if you know what I mean. Living for the minute on a river boat queen. I work all day and play all night. Wake up in the morning, gonna feel alright. No, I ain't got time to talk. You won't see me run. You won't see me walk, because I take the boat where I need to get and if I ain't been there, then I ain't there yet.

-Endless Friendship-

I want to try a lot. I want to try everything. I don't know who you are, but you look like a friend to me. And I know we don't have long to go, down the road, before we see the light. Watch them rise and fall. In the dark of the night, I will heed your call. I want to see your face light up the morning sky. You put me in my place and I don't know why. And I know we don't have long to go, down the road, before we see the light. Watch them rise and fall. In the dark of the night, I will heed your call. And I know we don't have long.

-Road Kill Blues-

Dead 'coon on the side of the road, lying next to
the flat dead toad and someone must have hit that
cat. He's lying next to the cold dead rat. Beside a
poor, dead puppy dog who's lying next to a dead
groundhog. There's a dead fox and a dead
squirrel, a dead rabbit and a dead turtle. And
around about this time of year, you're bound to
see a few dead deer. And if you do run out of
luck, can you smell that old dead skunk? And if
they don't end up as someone's meal, they might
end up under someone's wheel. So keep an eye
on each path you choose or you'll end up with the
Road Kill Blues.

-Prayer for Love-

Where, oh, where has my baby gone? She's gone,
oh Lord, and it won't be long. When will I see the
light? When will I know it'll be alright? Why, oh,
why am I feeling blue? I'm wasting each moment,
these times without you. When will I see the
light? When will I know I can call you mine?
Now, I know that I must be strong and find a way
to carry on. I don't want to be alone. Where, oh,
where has my baby gone?

-Spring Rain-

It's in the way that she comes to me, like the love of the mountains. It's in the way that she calls to me, like the sound of the spring. And the rain falls down and washes over me. I look at her and she smiles at me, that's when the waves start rolling. A light that grows ever brighter, across an endless sea. I stand with her, beneath this water falling over the sands of the Earth and catch a glimpse, within a kiss, of the morning sunrise. And the rain falls down and washes over me.

-Mountain Soul-

I've been roaming these hills about all of my life. I've seen the waterfalls and the mountainsides. A little bit of country, if you can understand. When I was a child, I owned all of this land and now time has come and gone like the whisper of the wind, like a sweetheart memory, like a good old friend. The mountain is in your soul. The dusty old trail leading to the fishing pond seems so awful lonely since the day that you were gone. I sit and think about the dreams my grandfather built. He said, think about your life and take care of yourself. Now, that he's gone and I go on alone, I have faith in myself and I know where I belong. The mountain is in your soul. Sitting by the creek at night, I count a million stars. I have no need for the city lights or the moving sound of cars. A little bit of country, if you can understand. When I stand on this mountain, I will stand for what I am and when I fly away and I leave it all behind, you know, I will find my way and I know what is mine. The mountain is in your soul.

-Scores of Pain-

When I met you I swear the ocean set on fire. Even the limbs on the trees would bend to my desire. The earth gave way to an everlasting light, while the wind waged a war on an invisible fight. The sound of devastation and nourishing love. The sight of a lion lying next to a dove. A silent compassion of a cleansing rain. A song of triumph through scores of pain. When I came to, I found an interesting sight. All I could see was there for me every day and night. The city was crying with shame and the train was running late. Even though it all stays the same, everywhere you see another brand new change. We just keep moving along, to the sound of the song, through the scores of pain, until we find the time to decide what we've got to do. We've got to make it right. Bustling down, underground, the lights go by as the world goes 'round. Catch a ride to the other side of town.

-The Way I Love You-

I love my life. I love my family. I love this world. Yeah, it's the place to be. I love my girl, like I'm supposed to do and I love the way that I love you. I love my pain. I love my enemy. This may sound strange. Yeah, but it has to be. There is no shame in what I'm going to do, because I love the way that I love you.

-The Boundary-

I never get the words out fast enough, but I'll try this time…here it comes. All fear is relative to our death. Compassion. Reliving the moment. Forgiveness. Wherever you are. See me silent and thus you know it. Meaningless words simply misunderstood. No-one knows and yet they feel it, share it and cannot deny it, cannot find it and live the way they shine. My account is natural. No machine. A never-ending dream. No math. Just a feeling. You might be energy. A step beyond everything. Hiding below the silver sea. Still there even in darkness. That is why. That is how. Can you see? Not with your eyes, but with your mind. The silent song we all sing. The secret of a diamond ring. No dimension. No road. No lines. Not even stars. Just the sky and just the sea.

-No Escape-

Well, you're on your way down an endless track. You only hope that you don't make a mistake. There is no way of going back. There is no way to escape from the pain in your heart. On another day, when you're looking back, you will think to yourself and you will say, there is no way of going back. There is no way to escape from the pain in your heart.

-Neurological Implants-

We have an expression of our own we cannot fake. We meet as chords in the words of impact. Live the life. How your heart has crossed the line to find the bottled up verse. Mountains filled with sand, eyes closed. So clear is the water. The hand in the voice. We are living on water, stagnant with sympathy. He doesn't understand what it is.

-Giving-

Love's eternal shadow. Silence of brilliance. A door to another side. Yet revealed more real. Comfort inside the smallest reason. The simple way of knowing. Not to capture, but to catch you when you fall. Share a smile and look upon the outstanding beauty of being and giving. Giving gives back in many ways. The wind moving gently upon the bank and the water's soothing trickle. A hint of light upon the rocks. Green moss covers the trees and vines hanging in the branches. Birds in the distance call to one another in the stillness. Slowly they move closer and meet in a nearby tree.

-Freedom of Expression-

Only what I create. A trace of life upon the page. Insight to your mind. We are all part of each other. Expression is the only interpretation. Inside the mind is woven in strands of thoughts through time, all affecting reason and freedom of expression. *So* many questions. *So* much is relative. What you see is what you will find. Reaction is your contribution. Reflect to recognize. Collaborate, don't discriminate. Create, interpret and carry on with your lives. Freedom of expression is a love to defend.

-Free to Fly-

I was dancing at a party with a beautiful young lady when suddenly she was glowing with an immense light, shining within her. Everything was dark, but her radiance and the moon overhead. I look around and barely visible are others dancing almost in ritual, but I am only engaged with the presence of this lady of light. The more I focus upon her, the more everything else disappears, until we are both completely immersed within the dream. All becomes clear for one shining moment. Everything we ever dreamed or imagined became real for an instant, which quickly became the whole night. Reliving this feeling in amazement. I dreamed of marrying this woman and raising kids in the mountains. I look her directly in the eye with all attention and ask her if she wants to fly. We fall asleep and dream together. We are running through the forest at night as fast as we can, with ultimate anticipation and suddenly the ground is gone. We soar over a cliff and over the trees and fields below, gradually climbing higher into the sky until we gather in the clouds. We pause and she looks frightened. I grab her hand and all seems disarray. When the clouds give way we are back at home in the mountains. It's a beautiful sunny day. The kids are playing. The garden is growing. Another day. Our dreams are real.

-Surroundings-

I believe that your initial surroundings are playing an important part of your life at that particular moment in time. Each piece to the puzzle, with their own idea of the masterpiece. But, for one, individually when you look to the eyes that surround you, what do they tell you or how do they influence your life? When I see it in you I am forced to seek to try and understand that reason for my place there. Without reason I enter, but when I leave, I leave with a little more wisdom. In your eyes I see no closure. What do you seek and what does my influence have, on what lies beyond eyesight, for you? Here we can enter endless dreams. The dream is what holds us together. Anything that we imagine can be brought into a little more light and some things become real. What led us here to believe the dream of being together? Where you are together and you cannot deny it. Singularly, it can only be imagined, but through thoughts and dreams comes reality and all I try to achieve is reality. Focusing on what feels right and acting on it. You cannot deny certain emotions and some aspects of this dream are not as clouded as they seem.

-The Eagle must Land-

Fly high. Like a bird, pass on by. Fly high. In one word, I say, "Goodbye." You must find a destination. You will need a helping hand. Know there is no limitation, but eventually the eagle must land.

-Fill in the Space-

Run away, endless days, unseen. Calling to water. Quite a cluster of infinite galaxies. Birds fly. A bee's wing. Detail never fails. Docks and sails. A movie goer's lonely theme. Unreal, surreal dream on the television screen. Backstage commentary. Just a nook or a cranny. Space beyond the scheme of things. Controlled by the keys. Sense by far and measure. Slow the process to simple times. An easy go breeze. A natural high and the blind can see. When moments don't last so long things can be funky. Skip and slide your way through time. Never look back and leave no trace, a change or pattern. Just a taste. The bigger picture is what we create. Fill in the space.

-Revolution-

Things are never as they were before. Change, sense, the tide of morning. At a final point of no rationality. Senselessness. Motionless. A quest without question. Lying on the ground in full embodiment. Dream what things might be. Revolution. Around again. Things seem brighter. The wind moves higher. Time does not exist. Life is more of moments and now is all that really matters. What you do from that moment moves the moment. Revolution. Because all things have similar patterns, as do all things change.

-My Guitar-

To what I owe. A magnificent attempt of achievement. No reward, but my own creative smile. Unique, all things create. To what I am. You become your instrument. Accepting your achievements. Release. Over-wide exposure. This gentle wave sent freely. Of that which you can only see, infinite possibilities lie in between. Everything is known in itself to be unpredictably sufficient. Contemplating inward decisions of outward actions, through time, that distinguish signature appearance. Gathering to a single point to prove its uniqueness. There. Concepts of future relations circulate to life's pattern of brilliance. To what I believe. The truth stands out. What else do you see?

-Link-

A fearless ride into the never-ending cycle of time. Wrapped in every color, exploding in slow motion. Sliding over transparent waves that ripple forever. Echoes of light and brilliance, surrounding entire worlds of living beauty. Cascading through infinite dimensions of every thought, for each entity. The primary force. A connection between all things. The link between two worlds. A leap through time. Shuttered by smoke and a gentle haze.

-Leaky Roof-

Years spent wandering. Worst of all, it is all a surprise. Awakening to realization. We walk beast of men in a path not known to us. Forcing these simple rituals until they become complex manners of speaking. A formula in some distant language. A desperate search for an answer leaves a horrendous wake of wondering. The hopelessly unattainable. Striving to obtain something which is not even there. The final awakening. The evidence of subtleness. Only a short glimpse of existence. But there it becomes profound. For that is all that we know.

-The Lonely Rider-

A dark silhouette, in the mist of the morning, on top of the highest hill. Catch a glimpse of the lonely rider. Lord knows where he's been. Lord knows where he's been. A mountain of dreams that lead through the valley, carried by the wind. Riding alone and living the wonders of all that could have been. Call his name and no-one will answer and no-one can call him a friend. Riding the hills, provided by the master. The workings of his will. The workings of his will.

-Think to Yourself-

Think to yourself. What is your mind? Unlawful is the mind because in the mind one can do anything. An endless field of freedom, all in the thoughts of one's own consciousness and all of what surrounds it. Trying to interpret this is difficult for some, impossible for others, but there for those who know no limits and entwine everything around themselves. Listening, imagining, to see the world anew.—Elements of design. Color, texture, space, shape. Harmony between the elements causes unity. Simple standard principles we often take for granted. Every breath of life that is taken is also shared. Look of all. Answer your own questions. How would you answer? Be sure to complete your answer.—I was barely awake. The clock said 3:00 A.M. Drowning in sweat I sway over to the bed, collapse there and think uncontrollably. Unstoppable revisions flash throughout my head. Each thought, a leap through space, like pouring water jumping back against my face, forcing me to stay awake, though I am drawn to my sleep. I suddenly realize that I am being flung and tossed around the room, spinning. There is a very strange sensation in my head, like a dense pressure. I am conscious enough to be fully aware of my surroundings, but it feels as though I am in a dream, turning over and over. I see many things before me, but they go by so fast that it's hard for me to keep a fixed image long enough to remember. I can't remember what I am remembering. I see my birth, body and soul. I feel every emotion at one time. Somehow I control it and rebuild it slowly in my mind. Believing in myself was the first step. While it begins to come and flow evenly together, until I'm almost there.—I am awakened by a large buzzing in my ear. I look around and see that the clock says 6:30 A.M. All looks the same, but I feel influenced strangely somehow.—A flaming fire, becoming new. Strength is gained and proven to be sufficient, but loneliness is all around. The random messages, what do they mean? There is a blurring sound around my room. Voices calling through music, spreading over me. I feel as though I am floating, motionless, unable to move myself. All throughout my body I feel, what seem to be, tiny pins and needles being injected, numbing me completely. My heart beats faster…faster…faster, until I can't take it anymore. Suddenly, I am forced upwards into a pool of water. I wait and watch as I pull myself off the floor. The atmosphere, moving like liquid. What's going on? I wonder, when will it end? I strain to control myself as I feel the ground give way beneath me. Left behind, wandering until the morning.—As I walk down the path of knowledge I leave myself behind. My mind, an overwhelming bliss of feelings. Waiting alone, I sense no understanding of life in this world. If I need a destination I will find it. Again, I leave on my own path of acknowledgement. What is the purpose? I need not explain. I walk beside myself and cannot stop laughing. Why do I do, what I do, when I do it? Asking why, you'll never know. You must advance to it. I'm afraid…afraid of extinction. I feel as though I am balanced with annihilation. I wander on and search for enjoyment, to feel at ease. Reacting alone.—I felt sick to my stomach as I turned to see this large glowing light. The light grows bigger and bigger, for hours it seems, but no escaping the presence of this brightly immense light. Chills run through my spine. My hands go numb. My heart beats faster. Do I want it less or do I want it more? If only I could find a haven for my soul.—You must have a ground rule to understand. Millions of people, burning with innocence. They walk unknowing, lost to their self or self-meaning. Where can you find it, this meaning of life? Confusing and complicating. Thinking so hard, but wasting so much time. Like two people arguing, when they are both wrong.—Believers, running like children to know and learn what cannot be used. Deep within the thoughts of others lies a sanctuary of nothing. To be is nothing. To want to be is nothing. To believe is everything. Think to yourself and understand it all over again. Why is the sky blue? Why is the grass green? The only way to know is to believe. Wisdom can only be obtained by believing in great knowledge. Learning, adapting, changing the course, filling the gap, taking the balance, exploring time. Life is worth living only if you find out what life is worth living for. Find what your mind has, for you are the only one who can use it. Listen to the words of all. Act upon opinion and reason with the consequence. Believe that your words have strength. Find truth between the idolized universe. Make your understandings available to reality, to access and use willingly. Become a person of true righteous knowledge. Believe it.

-Stream-

The sun shines. The air is warm. Over the valley, a flowering city. The summer times. In days we dream. Over the many and so many more. The falling of water and into the stream. A wind that winding, sent whirling and swirling and quietly whispers and softly answers. Sometimes, with words we say. Alive, in ways we see. A hidden place, but there the same. Awakened up, by anytime or even so. The more you see the more you know it and on we go.

-The Joys of Life-

Set all of those who follow you afire and the castings will nourish the earth. A fertile field of a dreaming whisper, that cascades the flood, which devours our soul. Harness the forgotten wind and sail through the sky. Drive them deeper into thought, until the pressure suffocates any doubt within and only passion remains. A thread of needlework fabric that blankets the world with the unity of salvation. A mindless intervention. Calibrating. A destiny you cannot seek, but can only lead. For those are the words written down. Continuing. To feed the weak and breed the strong into inevitable confrontation. To sow this seed that lies within the heart of a screaming vessel. Because freedom stands alone. I see no institute for freedom, but an open door to a life of unlimited feelings. To feel the world struggle to be strong. For we are the voice of the Earth. All the pain and misery thrives in all of us, along with the gift of living the joys of life.

-See it All-

Somewhere, out in the darkness, in the shadow of a moon-lit sky. Hear the sound of the wind on the mountain. See it all in the blink of an eye. Endless sea, of an endless voyage. Companies, of an endless time. As you walk all alone in the darkness. See it all in the blink of an eye. No more thought and no more reason. Feel the change of the wind in the season. See it all in the blink of an eye. Roll on, until the wheel unwinds.

-Buried Treasure-

Streaming down upon the street-lit palaces and simple realities of living in a calm crevice. Small, yet always expanding. In all sounds that can please. The ear arrives in tune and perfectly clear and not a cloud showing could even be near. Just then, as we wake from the daydream together, we never forget where we buried the treasure.

-One More Time-

Joining in with the sound, take a look around and nothing will ever hold you down. Look around at what you see. How hard could it be, to just believe in what you see, when you know not everything is ever what it seems to be? Now, send your boat off to sea and you found a mountain to climb, but it seems so high and every step you take might seem like mistakes, but nothing will ever hold you down.

-The Good Old Days-

You wake up in the morning to see the sun rise above your head. The day has begun so you take off and run. You can go...anywhere. How many times have we crossed the same lines and how many lives have we lived? All we need is some peace in our minds, a time for love and to forgive. And when the sun goes down you try to slip away, to one of those good old thoughts, of one of those good old days. And when you stopped to hear the music play, what did you hear the music say? You wake up in the morning to see the sun rise above your head. All your dreams and thoughts are alive and real and love is…everywhere.

-Defined to Signify-

We are born to live and then to die. Softly, how everything moves by. How awkward all things may seem. The wind blows while dreamers dream. Refined to dignify.

-Old-

There is a peaceful place inside us all, between sleeping and waking. Waking to remember why we are dreaming. Dreaming to remember why we are awake. For a while it seems to be drifting thoughts, refusing to assure serenity. Meanwhile, experience is taken to be hovering above knowledge. With horror-filled eyes, the girl stares at the scattered, blue wreckage. She is astounded and cannot grasp its meaning. Listen to the echoes of silence. She remembers the joys of today brought this pain of tomorrow. A young man. A devil's head. A painted design. No hurry. Gently drifting. Another name. Another piece of the painting will be added.

-Frayed-

A filter of magnitude, created as an output for energy. Surging power for silent warriors. They are drawn by messages of captured freedom. Sentenced by angels. Awakened by dreams. A silhouette of light in darkness. A shade of standard decisions. Before night would change them, all be forgotten. A reward, less rewarding. Faceless shadows. Eternal mornings. Changed to form a different world. Shifted to incompetent beholders. Buried in their anguish, below their souls, one awakens. Words fed less below the winds.

-Songbird-

Glide along, songbird, and sing to your hearts content. Where we seek knowledge in all that we speak of. Sometimes you cry over things that are done and ones that you love. Endless is forgiveness. The effect is the feeling. Even if silently, the outcome of possibilities is unknown and infinite. Describing infinity only complicates it more. Ensure reality. Your awareness. How focused you are in your life. Sometimes you cry for what is to come. Calm yourself, songbird. Soothe your worried soul. Sing of all the good old days. Speak of them in every way. Rise up and look ahead. Every road is uncertain.

-Realize-

The wings of a bird, flapping. The dreams of words, tapping. The ghost of man, laughing. Angry men with liquid skin. A mother's love. A father's sin. Wooden souls and plastic friends. Hate to realize. Pages torn. Battle worn. Shadows of selfish reasons. Drawing of separate regions. Fragile symbol of morning. The dream is over-flowing. Hate to wake, but…remember to realize.

-Run Away-

She's the queen of my heart. Know our love will never part. Meet me in the morning. You know we'll run away and catch that setting sun. With you, I know we'll find a way. Meet me in the morning. We'll find a brighter day. Take me to the city. The wheels go 'round and 'round. Can you feel the river flow on the other side of town? Nothing stands in our way. I know our love will find a way. Meet me in the morning. You know we'll run away.

-My Only Hope-

Love, oh love, sweet love. It's the kind you only dream of. But love can be, oh, so real. Can you see the way you make me feel? The sun, the moon, the wind and rain. Through all the pleasure and the pain. We'll soar across the land and sea. Can you see what you've done for me? I need your love to help me grow. A guiding light within the snow. There are many things that I don't know. Can you see you're my only hope?

-Blind-

It's easy to close your eyes, forget your lies and remember why you are here in the first place. But if you try to wake up, the sun will blind you and all of your realities will come true.

-Reach the Shore-

Time keeps turning, that's for sure. This endless fight we're fighting for. To find a way, to get away, until the day we reach the shore. The sun, the moon and the stars. The best, the worst or something far away. In the forest, a danger lies. In a field, a sun that shines. In a cave, a voice that cries. In the sea, the answers why. Time keeps turning, that's for sure. Just keeps on rolling more and more. I must find a way, to get away, until the day we reach the shore. Just what are you looking for, today?

-Born Again-

Born again restless hand that feeds the knowers and doers do you die? Feelers do you feel? And those who dawn within the light. Tired helpless hand that holds the weary breath of birth and life.

I've got forty dimes to go and I'm on the train back home. Spent time all alone. Wishing bottles in a row. God, save me. A chair set for you. Carried me away. Fool, tame your senselessness. Wasting time to rest. Alone in the wistful wind. I ponder where it all began and so I stand again.

-The Fruits of Life-

An innocent hand, holding onto what's left. A dream is starting over. The mountain fell and is rebuilt again. A thought crossed my mind and quickly faded away before I could grasp it and then, when I least expect it, another thought replaced it. What is dreamt and what is sought. What is planned and what is captured. The wind carries it away once you've found it. To keep us going. Improvements and lasting memories are the fruits of life. To dream or to do. To fly or to follow through. When you get there, realize it or you'll never know you were there. Struggle, force your way through time. Hold onto hope, for will is the strongest medicine.

-In the Sky-

I've been to the sweatshops, seen the faces sad
and long. No pay for hard work, the work I've
spent all day long. I'm leaving you alone, I say.
Must I be alone? Play my beat for you to sing. As
I awake, sing my song. I've reached that age, at
the end of the shore. See the eagle through the
sky to more and more and more. The summer
moon…pleasant around the lonely room. Thanks
to you, you fill the air. How hard I've tried. No
need to care. In the sky…born so high. My life
gone by. What you see should never be so much
for you to ask me. What's yours cannot be sold.
Stay with me and grow old. The land here
brought me the seed of peace. But baby, the pain
of joy will never cease. In the sky…born to fly.
Don't ask me why you only find lies. In the
sky…I've found what really makes you cry. To
share my laden mind. Open up my closed eyes.
My tears fall on the ground. It helps her to grow.
She rolls herself around so that I will know how
far she really wants to go. Open up your needs to
me. Tell me…in the sky. Share me in your eyes.
Your love is too high. When I fall on you I see
the second time.

-Arise-

I'll sit down. Someone in the mirror told me when a sun explodes, the Earth will drown. When I'm alone, I will be found. Where'd he go? I'm still around. I can separate out the sounds. The brightest star that shines. No spoken word could express how bright it is. Laughter filled with sighs. A look within the eyes of morning. I'll arise.

-Life Dream-

As simple symbols set in stone. Under cover of darkness the child will dream. There he goes and no-one knows the end of it. He goes to thank his mother, his giver. He sees the image of his father, another page he burns. He takes one step further…into endless worlds of wonder. A rise of dreams upon his heart. A silent breeze of memories. Remember these as you awake and the journey begins, the never ends and I hold you in my arms. Outside and over my head. The silence of what has been said. I look into your eyes, we've finished our goodbyes and I fall asleep. The moon offers little light. Enough to see right through the night. As the child steps into dream.

I've found an opening of thoughts and lots of things, of life and of dreams.

-A Battle Song-

Scattered creatures on a world, displaying features with their words. As they listen to a song, leading them away, as they sing along. A commanding blessing, to speak openly. As we sat around our table, they spoke of victory. But there is a story in every word. Another man's message hidden within his sound. A few were walking, many were dead.

-Bound-

A dust filled meadow, gazed upon, under a shadow. As the wind blows, I watch the trees flow back and forth. It is coming from the north. Our day will come. Our day was born. Are you ready to go? Relaxing in a troubled reunion. A glass between us. Remarks, occasionally writing. Separated, but dedicated. A chance for hope in the pattern of a rainbow. Collapsed confusion, delusion and a fiery situation. A distant destination. Dreams of a future, of past feelings. There's a cat on the ceiling. Nestled with the hidden meaning. The wind is screaming. I am bound.

-A Free Ticket-

I said to me, "It's only a dream and there's an Earth and on it's you and me." I said to her, "You're lonely in my dream. Why don't we leave and find the sea?" I said to her, so desperately, "I think I heard you calling me. Just say the words and we can be in a world, so free."

-Let's Go See-

Well, you know it's time to let go. Look and see life along the open road. The feelings pass. The memories are told, to show the paths we have rolled. Take another look at yourself. Take another book from another shelf. It's times like these, oh please. Look, a boy so young, a man so old. The feeling is underneath. Possible pasts, of what you could be and between now and then, where did we begin? Or when did it become clear to see?

-Mountain of Dreams-

On a mountain of dreams, an open horizon of endless reasons. Raise your head, child, and look to the sea. Pick out the stars of possibility. Open your eyes to see what can be seen. The further you fly the closer you are, but the end, my friend, will always be far. And what's to come and what is to be? I stand beside of you and you beside of me. So let us leave this mountain behind and fade away into the sky. Realize our dreams are real, ours to hold and ours to feel. The time will come to turn around and look around at what we've found, standing strong on sturdy ground, to stay. And what's to come? And what is to be must be. I stand beside of you and you beside of me.

-Purple Leaves-

She is my question without an answer. I love her and I understand her. She is my mystery throughout my maze. She is my wonder. She is my gaze. Longing to love her, I won't fade away. I always need her. She is my everything. I sing to the rain. A long time since then, but my thoughts remain the same. My, oh my, how we've changed.

-Glory Day-

In the glory of the day, I found a love so real. Take what you feel, then get on your way. Tell me your secrets you hold so deep. Let them escape you and your life you'll see. It is yours and always will be. I don't know. You'll have to see. That's what'll keep us together, just you and me. Take what you feel and then tell me what you see. If you always fail at first, if at first you don't succeed, just try, try again. Try again for me. Believe in what it's worth. Believe what you'll see. Only you will know it. You don't have to take it from me.

-The Duel-

I once was a wandering boy so lost, who entered the season of the frost. Unprepared, unaware of the fortune bestowed upon his head. To find a woman he already knew. To take her challenge, to fight the duel of the quest of life. His reward, her love. With signs of spring, of unending things, forever and around again. His will, her shield. A fight 'til death, just to hear her sing and taste her lovely breath.

-Appreciation-

We wait until the morning light, to say goodbye as I hold you tight. Undecided, I can't seem to find the words to describe what I feel in my mind. My heart is lonely and you reached out to show me what my heart might want to find. Can you hear the birds singing, as the sun starts to rise? I can feel a new beginning. You have opened up my eyes and everything has a meaningful feeling. I just want to thank you and I don't know how. You turned my life around somehow. Things seem so much better now. The day was so much brighter. Even the people were a little nicer and this was all because of you. Somehow, out of everyone, you knew. All I can do is thank you, thank you, thank you!

-A Sense of-

A clear note, a crisp tone, a sense of a certain sound, distinctly heard. Rendering silent, an ear to hear. Receiving wonder along with familiar comfort and stern reminders of every classification, stored on every shelf. Releasing random interaction with awareness. To bring sweet surprise and a new foundation. A chosen selection, so fast, it's done before you've even

chose it.   An inquisition of
remain content and re-gather p
each cloud ever so slowly n
laughing and leaving on this plat
us.   Blue shades, transparent.   L   ıl
shadows of texture.   Constantly reliev   serene
battle scene. A signature, written by a cream. We
felt it. What a bright red ruffled dawn, a sense of.

-To get her-

Awaiting there inside her eyes, I am there with my
arms spread wide.   A sweet rhythm can fill my
ears, every time you come so near to me. Is there
the whisper of the wind, of an urgent message you
will send, to find each other? Soon two will meet
to be together.   But there's a thin line between
forever and never. So call aloud for what you seek
and you may see it could be me who really loves
thee.

-Deadwood-

Dawn on one so flying about thee.   On, round,
rising above the trees.   In the clouds, bit by the
breeze. Oh, a wide field of green. A blue shadow
of me on the ground surrounded by a world, so

you've seen into the stream. A looking glass of everything. Reflections, sparkling. Fountains and springs. Slip away. Gone off to the mountains to stay and moving back against the waves. Bright rays that light the way. Down the trails and past the fences. Over a bridge, across the water. So swift among sleeves of grass. To the stone, atop the hill. By the deadwoods and the grain, flowing with the morning rain. A warm spring to suit you fine, while walking into a sign. A lovely lake, cool mist arising. Shallow, under pools that shine. Grazing and gazing all endless time, soon as the wheels unwind.

-The Fight-

Was the fight for a cause? Many men, they did fall. Who will fight back? Who will be strong? Fear, they did lack as they walked headlong into death. The sea has gone black from the sky up above. They wanted a reason. They fought without love. Shake, shake, the earth began to quake. Smile, smile, we're laughing all the while. After all, it will all be over soon.

-Thunder Bird-

Thunder mixed with the day's rain. Under a fixed myth and a quiet flame, a bird is said to come down from the mountain, unheard and bound for some town. Falling further, hear her calling murder, fear or refrain. Shaking the walls, carving out halls in hollow hearts. Only the fearful, waking to shout. Two shallow parts, lonely or hateful. One deeper yet. Thunder mixed with the day's rain. We all get a little wet, just don't get soaked.

-Twilight-

Can you make the stars move? Words that speak so much louder than words. Someone speaks, while no-one is heard. The sound of one voice, stirring the herd. A blistering silence. The final word.

-Two Feathers-

Crystals and jars of all sizes. All gathered and collected and stored within the ice coated hills and floating, frozen beacons that ascend into the sky, like long strands streaming down on glazed shells that bend and reflect, as the light clasps every angle within and points to the very center of the Earth. Time is the space that fills the bottle. Flames in the street. A shadow on a new brick wall. A smile from a child. The hand that chooses someone for a special reason. The first ten years of your life. A growing building. A golden pyramid that reaches the sky and tells the moon why. A pair of feathers tucked in your pouch with care. You laugh at the times passing moment, which reminds you of something you don't understand.

-Ultraviolet-

Standing on color-coated leaves. Ultraviolet rainbows that lead to paths about, so close to see. Wondering who came so near, each time I glance unto the sea. Turning back to face my fear. Lights in houses. Homes in trees. Yes and no. Tall buildings show what sight a love could bring. No matter where, neither here nor there. Downtown, lights up the streets. All leaves turn brown and meet the ground, sliding ever so gently, down.

-Traphill-

Coming down, 'round yonder hill. You cain't escape a town like Traphill. As soon as you're coming down, you turn around and head back up to the mountaintop, to the tippy-top of Traphill. Coming down, 'round yonder hill. Ain't nothing like being in Traphill. You can stay all night if the fish don't bite, it could rain all day and the lightning strike, but you would stay there anyway. You're home in Traphill.

-Mountain River-

The mountain river. Rippling water, run, running clear. Calling the sun, the sun to come. In the morning we have begun...to shine. Hear us sing, of tales we bring, around the fireside. Of night-times that never die. All our cares we say goodbye. We'll dance and sing and laugh and cry. The mountain feels a rumbling sound of spring-time showers. How beautiful the time that we have to give. All we live, we live together, by the mountain river.

-Old Amends-

Where are we? I do not know. Into the light I'll go and pleasant dreams await normal nightmares. Ones where no-one can be trusted and everyone is right, but they can't explain it to their synthetic souls, ever to be forgotten. Forgot for what? The girl leaves me, it's alright. The rules will bend and blend, but do rules really bend in the end? If I can change them? I don't know. So what do you mean, "Bend if I can change them?" Again and again I savor the world. What I heard you say is absurd. We begin. It's a miracle. Open a window, so it's open. Just write it down, alright! Salivation glands, pouring the essence of all human annihilation. She won't talk. Continue…why? I wake up in the morning, turn the television on, I think about my wife, all my old amends. Back home, I wonder where my wife and kids might be?

-A Little Remarkable-

I guess I could explain it over a glass of wine, sharing my affairs by the fireside. Relaxed, bearing slowly, I lose my gaze into the never-ending cycle of time. Values, pouring dignity into my mind. You might recognize the pleasant sunshine on the eastern side of morning. But now, should you be swept in vain to find it, cast a glimpse into the old one's eye. Frequently you use her tools of magic, but only the feeble shall take the sailing mimic boat to the figure in the scene. Take this rusted little mind away! Glorified, just being a service to mankind. No aim, half born and still venerable. Dreary, the woman replants her child using the same worn out soil. Mud and dust echo a fragile cry in what old ones call it, an always ending sound of virtue. Human nature can be very severe, but it can be a little remarkable.

-A Single People-

Alone in the wistful wind, I ponder its beginnings. I stand within the vast few that many in their own right call, insight. Opening the many doors within our minds. I am pulled into the sky and between heaven and earth I leave the trail behind. I cross over a mountain and to a lake. As the leaves blow around me, a small voice proclaims, "A word is just one language. The mind is infinite." At that moment, through the elements of time, I looked into the lake and before me, as a dream I once remembered, was a large chariot. The driver of this chariot was you and you are the force that drives the world.

-Strange Things Begin to Happen-

Tired, helpless hand that holds the weary breath
of birth and past experiences. Portrayed as a new
and exciting substitute for freedom. We are not
forsaken. We have the power to control our
surroundings. A secret escape back into the
garden. Willows weep as a sign of pleasure. We
are never alone. We have found a home away
from home. Time to stop and think. Stop to
think of time. As we sit by the fire with our
drums and our instruments, as we sit here and
play, strange things begin to happen. And I look
up into the heavens and the rain fell down from
the sky.

-Shady-

I see now. The blue forest breeze. The words
caught with ease. A silence left remembering.
Labor is sent wandering. Another mind of
morning. A dream, stolen wild. An ancient,
laughing child. I concentrate on this page. As I
write the truth unfolds. A world sent haste-fully
watching. Friend, open your mind to share in this
brilliance. Dancing in trees, shadows balanced for
all to see and I count on its favors. I couldn't be
greedy.

-Bloating of the Soul-

Experience the expense of entangled enchantment. Arms are spread, open your eyes and fly. Fly to no-where and tell me what you see. Hear the distinct echo calling you home. Listen to the words for they can come true. But truth is an essence to us and is to say the least. Invite all who come. If they are willing, they too will share their dreams of the morning. Awake, a newness of life. Aware of all things and again speak. A shroud for the common welfare. Too indistinct and unheard of. Coolness in the summer air. Hair, flowing like a fountain. In the wind and back again. Beautiful to the blind. Cannot speak, but still they sing. Why all things want to ring. Unstoppable, can you call? To the river that goes to where no-one knows, but down the river you can find wholesomeness entwined. Together in the tree. Leaves fall and seek the wasting of time. How it mingles in the vines. The colors of the clouds astound me. But I am asleep to these things. Inside we sit and wonder why the bloating of ones soul astounds us. Wistfully taking away the amount of unity between two brothers. Until the dawn, we keep along, repeating the same unifying song.

-Deep-

I wished it would rain through my day, when nothing sacred can grow old. Only images whisper in my garden of dreams, so I can find flight through the breeze. Find shameless shadows on the wall, broken into it all. I wake so I can bleed. We rape the words and sell our needs. Defended on the stand. Fallen from the rose. Two born make a whole. I run through the field of forgetfulness. By the bay, the sea cries loud for help to reach the sky. No more to know. Deep, into the end it flows. Follow the road so cold. Breathe water, too blind to fear. Scream softly, so I can hear. Clouds listen. They teach to believe. Away today, inside to hide. The mountains of selfish night brought death to all for sight. Days laced with envy. The conductor of his lonely train cries loud with no face. Climbs dormant into space.

-Dying Embers-

Scattered ashes. Dying embers. The wind still catching on. Cries of the night. Alive, with the light of the moon. Calling out shadows. Foretold in the silence. A tremendous sound, causing the Earth to be still. Like a whisper, crashing through the forest. A bitter weep, to endure relief. A split second thought, to seal it with the grief. Awakened by the suns extending arms. A laurel light cascading the world.

-The Shell-

She tore her way into my soul, leaving me empty and alone. Leading me on with lies and quick decisions. Floating on clouds of mystery. A flickering uneasy sense of speed. Wavering like a mad wind. With self-destructing vengeance and merciless action. Lost to remorse and resentment. A thin shell of reason. Broken, only to feel the pain of this world. Seeping in through doubt and hopelessness. Shine forever, light of love. Busting, breaking through. Breathe in life, the world anew. With it is all the love you seek. Hold it for as long as you can. Live again and never look back.

-Give it a Try-

Give it a chance. Give it a try. Don't know what it is, but I know it feels right. I know it when I see the look in your eye. You know I got to have it, got to give it a try. Take it from me. It's easy to see the reason why I love you, you set my soul free. I only want to be right by your side. Close enough to grab it, got to give it a try. It's not too late. It just can't wait. Got to get together, now, what do you say? When I say I love you it ain't no lie. You know I can't take it, got to give it a try. Try for me. You will see. We will find. Peace of mind. Try and set me free.

-The Raging Sea-

When you come to me you're always crying and I always leave you with a smile. You know you just can't hide it from me. It's been such a long, long time. You, to me, are a mystery, as wild as the raging sea. I give my love to you for free, so you can find some peace in your mind. Rest, clear your head. I will hold you 'til the storm has passed. Open your eyes to the sun and rise with your arms spread wide. Love your friend as hard as you can. When I fall, will you help me stand? When I cry, will you dry my tears? When I'm afraid, will you calm my fear? When I'm alone, will you come on by? When I need you, will you show me why?

-Bird Shadow-

By the road. Down by the hill. Down by the water. Sitting alone. I look afar, over the river to see the shadow of a bird dancing on the water. The bird flies over me and into the sun. The wind picks up to push the trees enough to shake the leaves onto the water. I watch as they sweep away with time. I think some more about the wind and then it blows again. Cool and quick. The sound of the wind and the water fit so well together. Rolling rhythms with a gentle ease, in and out. And then the wind comes in to shout and slip away again. The bird still flies above the hill. He lets go when the wind blows. And I watch as he glides away. The clouds bring new shadows, the few that creep silently by. Bright, white clouds surrounded by a mid-day blue sky. In the distance larger clouds move closer, but I'll be gone after I sing this song.

-My Old Guitar-

One day I'll have a guitar that stays in tune. My old guitar is busted and only plays the blues. The neck is bent and the sides are bruised. The strings are rusted and I'm missing a few. But, oh, what the hay, I'll play it anyway and I just might play it for you. 'Cause, I know it ain't much and it's covered with dust, but it's the best old guitar that I ever knew.

-Long, Cold Highway-

A sleepless seam, without boundary, screaming down the street. Haystacks and old wooden buildings, barns and houses, filled with wants and needs. Parked at the graveyard. Pulling on your sleeve. Snug together on a long, cold highway. Waiting on top of the hill. Drive me wild. Drive in style. A smiling child. Walking along fences, fearsome and fearless. A witness to this endless request. Stopping to have a smoke. I picked you up in time to see the sun shine in your eyes. I put on my coat and I walked outside. Crawling through this cold weather, I guess.

-Dancing in the Tears-

Compromising, always sensitizing. A mesmerizing surprise. Meltdown in town. Swaying, weaving sand. Stand up again. Walking on wires. Rolling tires. Burning fires. Out of control. Window souls. Running. Flying back again. Close with comfort on a cold night. Somewhere in the firelight. Relieved, to find you in my dream. Dancing while I sing. Wash away the fears. Dancing in the tears. Redeemed. The endless sea of the light of day. I reach in and twist the Earth and spin until the monotony is over. Rendering, delivering silence as before. I felt you slip away from me, along with time. Where has it gone? Now, my shadows rest in doubt. Within, I let the secret shine.

-Mind Tribe-

The mind. A tribe. Singing, but the sound is screaming. As loud as they can before they slay the beast, devour their feast and make gods of themselves. A raging war that leads to the sea. The mindless follow heedlessly. Inspiring, amazing, and always entertaining. Relating. Calling the rain. The chosen planet. Pure with energy. Thunder, over the plain. Changing the way the mountain feels. A slow mist, rising through the field. Calm spirits of strange entities. Resisting the flood of time, transitions and realities. Approaching direction. Gaining speed. Living anywhere my mind lets me go.

-The Hunt-

The hunt never ends. It only begins with each moment in sight. A question of our lifetime. Struggling to survive from either side. Running down temporary lines, growing stronger. Before to wither, but not to waste away. Contribution to a moving system. A life force driven by the need to stay alive. Feeding the mind to buy some more time. Simple seemed to slip away into a test of strength and intelligence. A cultural defense. As we steal the air that we breathe, we eventually give back with no resistance. Forced along. Written down on your own time sheet. A world crying only because they don't understand their own self-indulgence and selfish needs. Gifts to replenish the sense of forgiveness. Not forgot.

-Omen-

I am the crow...a messenger of darkness by the light of day. A shadow in the sky. A reflection in the water far below, screaming higher. I am the owl...a warning by the fire at night. A silent destroyer and then gone. To perceive in the darkest places, listening. I am the rattlesnake...I am the end when you hear it coming. Shaking your soul free. Settled on the ground to find comfort and peace. A feeling.

-The Static Sounds like Rain-

I hear you through the wind. I see you through the ocean. I come to you in a dream. Our distance brings us closer. You seem so afraid, struggling to understand. You cannot perceive through the mist of clouds around your head. You have come to see me in hopes that I might heal your pain, but fear has no name. The static sounds like rain.

-Prime Time-

A prime diamond in my time. An ancient grove of treasure troves. Secrets, lies and deception. Illusions, delusions and misdirection. Black magic and fairy tales. Incantations and magical spells. A mystical land. A caravan. A tribal chant. A medicine man. A spiritual dance. A hypnotic trance. Unnatural dreams. A ceremony. The magic man. An Indian. A native culture. A primitive heritage. A custom of indifference.

-The Point-

A wasted object of perception. A silk remorse. A symbolic shyness. Away to the clouds. A way to the place where their crystal walls fell down. Shattering into a thousand year old stories. Told in the sunlight passing through stone. Clear as a bell. Clinging to the new found feeling of warmth in the evening. The mind sees things the eyes don't see. Captured by the impact fracture and written in the clay. Smell of the richness in bottom land. Rivers run rampant in the eyes of a flying bird. Flying to some unknown question. To spend the day looking down. You'd be surprised to see what your mind might find.

-Serenade-

I'm coming back home for the truth. Insane, the presence of youth, unchained. Gather all that is consciously made, to frame the day old rain. Rain filled with stars. To watch them march away. You whisper to me right as I fall asleep and I cannot help but dream. A serenade to sing. As if the rain knew exactly where to fall to cause this pain. Captured on the day of burning. Make it a memorial day. Make it in the month of May. So long. Such a scene of masterful material. A

building with imperial wings. Amidst. Against.
The mist around the oval table. The wind of a
fable. To see the sky turn grey. The old man
closes his eyes to recognize the dark. The
darkness of familiarity. To see what the light can
provide for our eyes. The rest is only in your
mind.

-Only for a Moment-

No-one ever told you what it all would take. No-
one ever showed you the paths we have to make.
I am free. I am free just for today. Only for a
moment, until that moment slips away. I only
want to hold you and take away the pain. I only
want to show you, life is more than just a game.
You are free. You are free just for today. Only
for a moment, until they try to take it all away.
No-one ever told you what it all would take. No-
one ever showed you the paths we have to make.
We are free. We are free just for today. Only for
a moment, until that moment slips away.

-Host of the Hoax-

The blue transparency of shadows entwined. All
o'clock. Slick, stick singer. Golden sophistication.

All aboard this shaking vesicle. Clogging the artery of investigation. A pirouette stable. A valet cage. Staging immense obstacles. The stolen hour. The imminent valor of intent. Soak up the edge of distant relationships. A desperate entity. This harsh remark of heartless measure. A canteen team of faceless endeavors. Wide cause of candy coated bear claws. Host of the hoax. Buttons and pairs of Indian hairs. In a row of red road flares. Enough to satisfy the taste, but not enough to waste. I hope to see you again in the light of clarity. For now, all I see is the darkness of curiosity.

-On My Mind-

You are my love and you'll always be mine. You are the girl who's always on my mind. Over and over, the years pass slowly by. But still I long to be right by your side. One thing you ought to know is how bright your light shows. One thing you never second guess, pick what is good for you and choose from what is best.

-Crystal Stories-

A chattering creek and the silver stone, telling their crystal stories. From a trade-wind in the south, to the clambering mountains under siege by the wrath of the mammoth storm cloud's malice. In spite of being sent from the sea, the rain can be so compelling. The sound of the tempest resounds. Waiting for the wind to ease and for the water to recede. Harvest the thoughts of purity. Deny the thoughts of delinquency. Where the air is clean and the sun slips away, sleeplessly. Lost in a sea of inequity, I see all things as they should be. The sun, falling in love with the ocean. Devotion to you each day. Dark clouds of rain. Dark birds flying away. Sweet smell of the ocean. A respectful scene. As the winds give way to an applause of redemption in a relentless rain.

-Angel in the Night-

My angel came to me at night. Time drifts away in a settling stream. The stone shows through the trees. Not a drop of rain, calling from the scent around you. Square lines meet parallel to mix in time, from one slight incline. Fusion, through confusion all around. Time is the illusion. Sitting on the rocks and stones. From the backbone, to the branches leaf tip, a giant ripple extends a substantial constant rhythm, reflecting the final extinction. Echoes of destinations. To categorize the implement of the enigma. To stand and follow among them and what description will they hold? A banner of the truth? The right to freedom? Co-existing is not an option.

-Filament-

Seat upon the proper element. The hands of time, reaching for the proper filament. A new sense of balance. An un-equal test of re-assessment. Gathering the perfect stones. Testing modulation. Fitting, formatting, before the waters rise again. I haven't seen the rain since I don't know when.

-Grocery List-

See what's shaking down. Show me all around. I got you on my mind. Can you help me out this time? Nothing else is making sense. I need your help at no expense. My brain drips out onto the page. No-one can control my rage. I see no reason, asking why. Sail what else into the sky. To help a crippled mind exist. And help me write a grocery list.

-Perforated Sky-

Look beyond the perforated sky. To rip intensions from your life. To hone the new trajectory. Replacing the old directory. A notice in the nick of time. The way opaque transcends the light. Let it slip away from you. To see the light behind the blue. A crystal color scheme. The gamut of all themes. The wind that winds throughout the dunes. A silent song inside a tune.

-One Moment-

Below the hill, sitting still, above the field. Atop a stone, playing a song, they sing along. As the wind blew, as new waves in the breeze, through the trees. The two sent walking. Laughing, caring, sharing, and talking. Pausing to capture the moments. To say, "This is how I feel today." When you sing your love will bring happiness wrapped in sun-lit rays. A last glance at warmth to end another day. Night will change words to stone, walking slowly home.

-Sebastian-

There's a dog they call Sebastian and that dog belongs to me. Every time I call his name, there he would be. Over the hill I see, he's waiting there for me. If I ever had a dog, Sebastian it would be. Oh, oh, my sweet Sebastian, Sebastian you are free. Free to run through a field forever, because free you'll always be. You belong, you belong to me. If I ever had a dog, Sebastian it would be.

-The Sun King-

The Sun King's shining armor reflects the light of our world. Signs, so discarded, to implement praise. Sincerity, to outward devotion. To accumulate into a rising prayer. To grow up and go on.

-Get Started-

Everything you ever had, you wanted. Everything you ever had is gone. Every time, you know, you think you get started. Every time, you know, they say you're wrong. I don't know. Where are we going to go? If I knew now, we'll make it through somehow.

-Lonely As Me-

Lonely as me, you'll never be. You are my flower. I am your bee. We'll get together. You will see, lonely as me. Lonely as me, you'll never be. I am a mountain. You are the sea. We'll get together. You will see, lonely as me. Why would you leave me? Why would you leave...lonely as me?

-Break of Dawn-

Gone, like the break of dawn. Gone, like the wind. Gone, like a river stone. No, I won't be back again. Gone, like a waterfall, like a train rolling down the track. Gone, like the break of dawn. No, I won't be coming back. You might think that I'd be so lonely, but I am free and free is the only way to be.

-Old Hollow-

I've got a girl and she's waiting for me and all I've got to do is call her. Then we've got to find a

place to meet. Maybe down in that old hollow. Well, she doesn't mind a little moonshine and a guitar on my shoulder. Because every time I play for her I only want to hold her.

-Forever and a Day-

Love for me, forever shall be, as long as you are. I can see your love for me lives within your heart. Sharing, caring, and knowing that your love is here to stay. Understanding, forever and a day. Let your love lead the way. Love will be for eternity, arms open wide. Love, you see, will never leave, always by your side. Sharing, caring, and knowing that your love is here to stay. Understanding, forever and a day. Let your love lead the way.

-Put it Down-

Put it down, put it down, lost my baby on the turn-around. When I turned my head, she was no-where to be found. Underground, underground, can you hear it calling from another sound? Will you face the wind or will the wind hold you down? Going to town, going to town, going to find my city, turn the city around. Until I find my baby I just can't put it down.

-On the Other side-

I don't know if I'm right, but I'm strong. I don't know if it's alright, but I'm already gone. I'll meet you on the other side, so long. I know that I cannot hide from the light any longer. I run beside the lion to the lake. I stare into the star-lit pool. As the lion drinks, the ripples become the pages of time. In them I see a new beginning. I'll meet you on the other side...

-A Hint of Love-

A little hint of love. A little hint of love. That's all that was. A little hint of love. Another day might not be the same. I wonder why I test my fate. Ain't no reason why. No, there ain't no reason why, but I've got to try and win your love. There ain't no reason why. Another day might not be the same. I wonder why I test my fate.

-End of the Rainbow-

There's life at the end of the rainbow. There's life at the end of your street. There's life wherever you go. There's life that you cannot see.

-Dreams-

Dreams, dreams, dreams. The candle-light it seems is flickering as bright as the sun, two are one and all things begin to cease. I've told you this before or maybe I was asleep. This is not the end, but a new beginning. I travel in the light and slip throughout the night to regain internal strength, as strong as I can be. I hope that you will see a tinge of blue beneath the tree, the mountain's view from under the sea, the golden sheath of an angel's wings, and the rays of light that stretch for an eternity. Dreams, dreams, dreams.

-A Thousand Years-

If I could show you how I feel, if I could show you how you lift me up into the clouds, you take me to a higher ground. Show me how you feel. Turn me around and around again. Show me how you feel. Turn me around for a thousand years. I could try to understand why, but I might never know. I could try for a thousand years to satisfy my soul. All I need is you to let me know. All I need is you to make me whole. Show me how you feel. Turn me around and around again.

Show me how you feel. Turn me around for a thousand years.

-A Little While-

I just want you to know that I love you so, but don't be afraid if I run away. I don't want to go, because I need you so, but please don't cry when I say goodbye, because I'll see you sometime. I just want you to smile for a little while, because when I'm gone it won't be long. I don't want to go, because I need you so, but I have to try and you know why, because I'll see you sometime.

-Who's to Say-

There is no right or wrong, just false and what is true. Who's to say what's right for me, may be wrong for you? But, every-body knows what love is and every-body has a friend and every-body knows there's a consequence to every little thing there is. Who's to say what price to pay? You decide what to do, today.

-The Banyan Tree-

Swinging from the banyan tree, having lots of fun, just you and me. Head on down to the old trout hole, better not forget your fishing pole. Try to make a fire most every night, if you ain't got wood, then you ain't got light. We wait in the dark 'til the morning comes, then we shine our light like the rising sun.

-Venture-

Find your way out of the dream. Look around at everything. Thank God, it's yours to be the same. You are part of everything. Death is black, you'll see so fast. But, wouldn't it be good if we could really make it last, even if our dream was one step out of our grasp? Determine what you know you can do, then venture out and see what life has for you.

-Ivy-

Ivy grows on me and I don't know why, but I can see her in my dream. Well, she's alright with me. She's as bright as can be and blocks out the world around me. Ivy grows on me. It's in her heart, in her smile. She covers me like a vine. It's in her love, in her mind and I don't know why, but I can see her in my dream.

-Slip into the Night-

A quiet slip into the night. A winding road where danger lies. A distant star, far away at first. A shallow moon covering the Earth. On the path of wonder, I try to forget, remembering yet, the forest surrounds me. The light falls through the trees and into my eyes, brighter with time. Drifting sounds stir me as I stare into the star-lit sky. Laughing as the strong winds blow. A silent cry from me, you know. You never seem to notice why. Look deep within the rolling tide. A quiet slip into the night.

-Love Letter-

I don't know how long, since my baby's been gone. I'll write you a letter. I'll sing you a song. We'll get back together, get to carrying on and live for the day, like our very own. But, you've got to give me a chance. My love is true and love's the true test, to rise above the rest. My love for you, babe, is the very best. Call me on the phone or just come right on. We always seem to find a way to make it through another day.

-Make up your Mind-

Baby, come and see me today. Yeah, I think I lost my mind. Tell me what it is I should say. No, I ain't going to lose you this time. No, I ain't going to lose you this way. I say believe in something true. Well, you know that I believe in you. Open up your mind and I know that you believe it too. Well, you know that was a beautiful thing that we had. Do you want to leave me this way, so sad? Don't leave. I know that you love me and I know that it's alright. Baby, won't you come and see me, tonight? Please, please, please, babe, you know you've got what I need. I ain't got much time and I ain't got too long. Make up your mind, babe, and tell me where do you belong? Please, please, please, come back to me.

-Open Road-

On the open road, an endless sea of light. Weather wind will blow, to make me feel alright. Time for me to go, driving into the night. Will I

make it on my own? In the end you'll know. On
the open road, it'll be alright.

-The Only Salvation-

How can you fly with no wings? When your hope
is carried so high? When your love is like the
breeze and there are so many questions in you
eyes? No-one can last forever. That's why they
try to stick together. My heart is slowly fading
into a star-lit sky. You stand as a mountain of
stone. With hard work and determination, it will
pay itself off in the end. As you are just a grain of
sand. My heart is light as a feather. Yeah, we are
all still together.   Alone in this dark place,
sheltered by a mother's love. May this soul find
its way, guided by a lonely dove, to its forgotten
haven. To be re-born again, the only salvation.
To be alone is not to be lost. When you are lost
you find freedom and you forget what you were
thinking.

-Petunia-

The same old road that I've been on a thousand
times. I live way out in the country where I can
free my mind and if you don't believe me, well

then, please don't think I'm lying. A girl like sweet Petunia is a girl that's on my mind. Well, she lives so far from me, but she could bring the mountain to the sea. The same old river flowing underneath the pines is rolling down the mountain to the ocean and the sky and if you don't believe me, well, please don't think I'm lying. A girl like sweet Petunia is a girl I hope to find. Well, she lives by the sea. Not nearly close enough to me.

-Izabella-

Izabella has found a fella and I can't make her stay. Every-time I bring her home she turns and runs away. I could hold her down with a lock and key, but that don't make much sense to me. She only wants to be free and that's the way it has to be. Oh, why do you leave when you know I've been so good? You've gone and found someone else and I knew that you would. Where have you been, runnin 'round for, oh, so long. Next time that I see you, I know that you'll be gone. Izabella, runnin free. Izabella, run from me. Izabella, come back home. Izabella, on your own.

-From the Heart-

Baby, won't you let me sing you a song. I'll stay with you forever if you sing along. All you gotta do is hear the tune that comes from in your heart. I'll sing a song about the look in your eye. How every-body wants to know the reason why. I'll sing a song that'll make you cry and a one to make you smile.

-Sweet Honey Pie-

Hey, girl, you gotta come see me with them curls in your hair. You know life is well worth living like a run through the town. I just want to spend time with you. Unwind with you, girl, that's all I want to do. Oh, while the sun still shines and the sky is blue, you are always on my mind, 'til the end of time.

-Sitting on Empty-

Well, the price is high and I'm running low and if I don't slow down I'm gonna run out of fuel. Yeah, the price is high and I'm running low and if I don't slow down I'm gonna run out of fuel. I had a quarter tank at a quarter 'til, by a quarter after it was time to fill. Sitting on empty, running on fumes, tell me Lord what should I do now? Help me out somehow. Well, the price is high and I'm running low and if I don't slow down I'm gonna run out of fuel. Yeah, the price is high and I'm running low and if I don't slow down I'm gonna run out of fuel. In the middle of the woods, in the middle of the night, any minute now, I think I see that light. Sitting on empty, running on fumes, tell me Lord what should I do now? I'm about to run out. Well, the price is high and I'm running low and if I don't slow down I'm gonna run out of fuel. Yeah, the price is high and I'm running low and if I don't slow down I'm gonna run out of fuel.

-Following-

All I see, all I do, all I am, is part of you. I spend my time, wasting time, to realize, I'm in disguise, alone. All I need now is to get out. Back again, coming in, following, and turning thin. I can't provide all the time. Asking why, I begin to cry, why do we all die? Where will I be tonight and will it be alright? I can't even say where I'd be today. I'm needed all the way. Follow me today. I know the way.

-Lost in the Day-

I'll meet you down by the sea somewhere. I don't know how, but I don't care. See them there all upon the shoreline. I don't mind that they don't understand. Drifting away. Silent, no-one hears. Lost in the day. Seems like many years. Seems like we've met here before. I don't know how and I don't know when. See them there still on the shore. Over the line, watch me fly, now. Wander away. Blinding light. Walking a strange way. Some-where, some-time, before now. To all who are and all who were here. To all men born and those who die and to those who live beyond the sunrise. For today becomes tomorrow and now becomes change. To see new light of a new day through the waking eye. To know that you're alive.

-Sleeping Love-

I sit beside my love, who is sleeping. Oh, how I love her so. I could sing about her until morning and not even let her know.

-Gypsy Clouds-

Over the mountain. Over the hills. Into the valley. Through the fields. Across the sea. To a barren land. Into a meadow and over the sands. They gather together to speak their words and tell their tales and fly away like birds. They fly over the mountain. They fly over the hills. They fly into a valley. They fly through the fields. They fly across the sea. They fly to a barren land. They fly into a meadow and they fly over the sands. They gather together to speak their words and tell their tales and fly away like birds. As they dance around to a wonderful sound, the smoke arises as their feet lift off the ground. Did you see them come? Did you see them go? When will you see them again? Now, they're just a memory. Gypsy-like clouds, changing their shape, changing their places on the wind. Coming around, who knows when? Maybe never. Maybe never again.

-Down the River-

Where the land rises from the sea. Caravan, carry me away. Ever grateful I will be, for every sign that shows me the way. To the mountain of the stone and the fountain washes all away and you know, now, where you belong. You go home, now. Carry me away.

-Every Waking Hour-

Stored throughout time. Day and night, we inch our way through darkness to find light.—It's hard to start a fire. If you do it catches on. But, you always have to feed it and it goes out when you're gone.—Dirt and leaves, through light shafts and passages. Growing mosses on oak wood trees surround the moat like scenes. Along the banks, wild red berries cling to the sides, as the swishing and soothing trickle sound of the water passes by your side.—The fire, still remaining, burning only as before. As you lay two sticks upon it and go looking for some more.

-Maple-

She's so fine. She's all mine. Sweeter than the summertime. She's alright. Clean out of sight. Hotter than a pepper plant. Well, she's holding onto me, just as strong as a maple tree. I'll take you where you want to go. Where do you want to go? Do you need a ride to the store?

-Dead Head-

I guess I'll never see your sea. I guess I'll never know your shore. I guess I'll never understand what I never understood before. But, I know that I must go and it's time to say goodbye. I'm headed for an open door into a never-ending sky. Think of me when you hear a tune, about a love that is coming soon, but slipped away with the wind before the blossom could bloom.

-Coming Around-

Oh, baby, keep coming around. Oh, baby, keep coming around. Oh, baby, keep coming around me. I know a girl who grew up in the mountains. She roams this land and she is free. It doesn't take long to track her down. She knows everyone that you meet in this town. Her hair is like the sun and her eyes are like the ocean. I ran with her into the light. She just kept going, until I couldn't see her. I walked alone on a cold dark night. Well, she is so kind that the world could only love her. But, she doesn't sit still for too long. She just keeps searching to find the answer, until a brighter day will come along. Oh, baby, keep coming around. Oh, baby, keep coming around. Oh, baby, keep coming around me.

-Dream the World Away-

Sitting on a bridge, just me and you, watching a sky so blue. You always make me laugh. You always make me cry. Watching the water roll by. Flow into the ocean, a never-ending sea. Our silent devotion, just you and me. Dream the world away, at least for one more day, to dream the world away. The mountain is singing for just me and you. Oh, what a wonderful tune. You always make me smile. I look into your eyes, watching the water roll by. Forever flowing into the sea. We must keep going, just you and me. Dream the world away, at least for one more day, to dream the world away. No time for sorrow. There's always tomorrow to dream the world away.

-Midnight-

By midnight, I'll have your soul memorized. Not only for you, but for my lonely eyes. I've found the ones who haven't failed to get it yet. Why can't you help me make it through, for you? It can be recognized by the shamefulness of my disguise and her love can't define why she aches for shapes in different colored signs. Beautiful and tangible, in awkwardly placed lines. The sea will rise, aloft, a moon set high and on the corner of the edge is where I sit and cry. I wait for midnight, when days are born to die. By midnight, I'll spread my wings and fly.

-Loon-

As we sat on the edge of the Earth again, we watched the rare loon feast. As I waited for them to join us for what we stand, my gaze was on the sea to the east. Leave my common sense behind. All sanctioned on the other side of the leaf. Fallen from the ancient trees to leave; leave me the air it takes to breathe. Light amend, into body lend. The spirits born from she. In this emptiness, old men wait to see, the lost in form, born free. To wait for death to wake me. I lost all my thoughts on the eastern sea. Cold in dark. Coming forth to save me the peace.

-Seraph-

So sweet how our eyes meet, how our smiles greet, how wild my heart beats. She is tearing me apart. I look at her heart when I see her face. How I long to hold her. How I contain these moments as memories to embrace. Her laugh can erase all the hate the world creates. How I long to kiss her and forget that I miss her. Does she know how I love her? Can she see how I see her? So sweet how our eyes meet.

-Liberate-

I walk to free my mind. I talk to the sky. I say, oh Lord, well, you've got to try and hold your head, hold it way up high. Well, you're the one they want. But, who are they to decide? I say, you've got to find your way to live your life. Well, there ain't no law against who you are. They'll never take away who you are. I say, you've got to make your way your only way to live your life.

-Pebble-

I'm standing on this pebble, a mountain of stone, looking at the valley below. I hold my arms so wide and smile to touch the sky. I know I've gone no-where, but only in my mind; I can touch the sun and watch the rising tide.

-Where to Go-

I sent out a letter, yesterday, asking why. Why won't you come my way? Or even try? Well, you can try to satisfy your mind, but you don't know where to go. So you go on alone. You carry on. You must be strong. Make your way, your only way. Satisfied by what you see. You're only too afraid to leave. Carry on sweet one. Catch the setting sun. Find the hand that helps your flower to grow. Let my love be your light in the snow.*

*CO-WRITTEN BY: CHAD LAUGHTER

-Your Love-

Your love will always be here. When I look into your eyes to see the sun brightly shining on a beautiful sky. So, I sing you a song about the moon or a star so high. Talk to your friends and say how much you love them. Open your heart to find yourself and free your mind from what you left behind.

-Sweetie Pie-

Sweetie pie...you know why. You're the spring in my step. You're the look in my eye. I'll never regret being kind to the girl who stole my heart. Honey bee...you are so sweet. You're the sound of the wind. You're the song of the sea. With you I never know where the hours go. Hello darling...hear me calling. It won't be long 'til the stars start falling. But, you know that I'll be there. You don't have to worry about me.

-Pick a Dream-

Pick a dream, like a leaf from a tree. Rob my soul. Run away with me. The sun is gold. The sea is green.

-Thanks-

Love in words or music played, of heartfelt feelings of life every-day, is yours, from me. So gratefully I say to you all...thanks.

-Last Words-

Think about things that are important in your life
and always take care of yourself.

Older and under the stars, the sea is much
brighter, tonight…